YASMIN

THE SEED OF AKHAND BHARAT

BY
BALAJI RAMAKRISHNAN

First Edition
2025
Chennai, India

YASMIN – AN ABANDONED BEAUTY

In shadows deep, where secrets reside,
Yasmin, a widow, with nowhere to hide. Just
twenty years, a life torn apart, Samir, her
son, a beat in her heart.

Her husband gone, a cruel, twisted game, Now
shadows whisper a dangerous name. An Indian
man, a Hindu so bold, A mission assigned, a
story untold.

Seduction's the weapon, her beauty the bait,
To betray his trust, and seal his fate. For
Samir's life, a fragile, small plea, Hangs
in the balance, for only she can see.

A web of deceit, with terror concealed, One
wrong move, and doom is revealed. Can she
walk the line, with grace and with fear, Or
will both she and Samir disappear?

The clock ticks fast, a relentless pace,
Yasmin's dilemma etched on her face. In this
deadly game, where love turns to ash, A
mother's resolve, in a desperate dash.

CHAPTER ONE

Bala, disguised as Riaz, stood out among the sea of pilgrims in Mecca. His eyes closed, hands raised in prayer, he sought forgiveness and guidance. Suddenly, a tiny voice pierced the air, "Help! Grand-père!"

A four-year-old boy, with piercing blue eyes and curly blonde hair, clung to Bala's robe, tears streaming down his face. Bala's heart melted as he knelt beside the child.

"Where's your grandfather?" Bala asked, trying to comfort the boy.

The child sniffled, "I...I lost him. We were praying, and then...and then I couldn't find him."

Bala's eyes scanned the crowd, but there was no sign of the grandfather. He took the boy's hand, trying to reassure him.

As they navigated through the crowds, from the boy's backpack Bala discovered that the boy's name was Samir, and he had come from France with his grandfather. But as the day wore on, Bala realized that Samir's grandfather was nowhere to be found.

A sense of unease settled in Bala's stomach. He knew that Samir's grandfather might be lost forever in the vast crowds of pilgrims. But he couldn't bring himself to tell Samir the truth.

Determined to help Samir find his way back home, Bala made a bold decision. He would travel to France with Samir, to reunite him with his family.

But there was one problem – Bala was traveling under a false name, and he had no documents to prove his identity.

Bala knew that traveling to France with Samir wouldn't be easy. He had no documents, and his false identity as Riaz could be discovered at any moment. But he was determined to help Samir find his family.

As they navigated through the crowded streets of Mecca, Bala spotted a small travel agency. He took a deep breath and stepped inside with Samir.

The agent, a kind-eyed Saudi man, looked up from his desk. "As-salamu alaykum, how can I help you?"

Bala hesitated, unsure how much to reveal. "I need help getting this young boy back to his family in France. His grandfather...passed away during the Hajj."

The agent's expression turned sympathetic. "I see. That's tragic. But don't worry; we'll do our best to help. Do you have any documents for the boy?"

Bala took the backpack from the boy and checked once again. "Yes and I'm willing to do whatever it takes to get him back home."

The agent nodded thoughtfully. "Okay, I think I can help. But it won't be easy. We'll need to contact the French embassy, and..."

Bala's eyes locked onto the agent's, a sense of hope rising within him. Maybe, just maybe, they could make this work.

The agent, whose name was Abdullah, quickly got to work. He made a series of phone calls, speaking in rapid Arabic to various officials. Bala watched anxiously, Samir clinging to his hand.

Finally, Abdullah hung up the phone and turned to Bala. "Okay, I have some good news. The French embassy is willing to help. They'll send someone to meet us in Jeddah, and they'll take care of getting Samir back to his family."

Bala's face broke into a wide smile. "Alhamdulillah, thank you so much, Abdullah."

Abdullah smiled back. "You're welcome, my friend. But we're not out of the woods yet. We need to get to Jeddah, and then we'll need to convince the embassy officials that you're telling the truth."

Bala nodded, his mind racing. He knew it wouldn't be easy, but he was determined to see this through.

As they made their way to Jeddah, Bala couldn't help but think about his own situation. He was still traveling under a false name, and he knew that if he was caught, he could face serious consequences and his task here was under questionable.

But for now, he pushed those thoughts aside. He was focused on getting Samir back home, no matter what it took.

As they arrived in Jeddah, Abdullah led them to a small café where they would meet the French embassy officials. Bala's nerves were on edge, but he was determined to see this through.

A few minutes later, a kind-faced woman with a warm smile walked into the café. "Bonjour, I'm Madame Dupont from the French embassy. I've been sent to help Samir return to his family."

Bala stood up, shaking Madame Dupont's hand. "Merci, Madame. I'm...Riaz, and this is Samir."

Madame Dupont's eyes widened as she took in Samir's tear-stained face. "Poor little one," she cooed, kneeling down to hug Léon.

As they sipped coffee and discussed the details of Samir's return, Bala learned that Samir's father had abandoned his mother, and she had been living alone in Paris. Samir's grandfather had taken him on the Hajj pilgrimage to help him cope with the loss of his parents' relationship.

Bala's heart went out to Samir and his mother. He couldn't imagine how difficult it must be for them to face the challenges of life alone.

Madame Dupont smiled at Bala. "Merci, Riaz, for taking care of Samir. You're a true guardian angel."

Bala blushed, feeling a sense of pride and purpose. He knew that he had made a difference in Samir's life, and that was all that mattered.

As they prepared to leave for the airport, Bala felt a pang of sadness. He would miss Samir, but he knew that the little boy was going home to his mother, where he belonged.

CHAPTER TWO

As they boarded the plane to France, Bala felt a mix of emotions. He was happy to see Samir reunited with his mother, but he was also anxious about his own situation. He had traveled to France under a false name, and he knew that he could face serious consequences if discovered.

But Bala's concern for Samir's well-being outweighed his own fears. He accompanied Samir to Paris, watching as the little boy's face lit up with joy as he saw the Eiffel Tower and he uttered that his mom took him there before.

As they arrived at Samir's mother's apartment, Bala's heart swelled with emotion. Samir's mother, a beautiful woman with tears in her eyes, swept Samir into her arms, thanking Bala profusely for bringing her son home safely.

Bala smiled, feeling a sense of pride and satisfaction. He knew that he had made a difference in Samir's life, and that was all that mattered.

As he prepared to leave, Samir's mother approached him, her eyes shining with gratitude. "Monsieur Riaz, I don't know how to thank you. You've brought my son back to me, and I'll never forget it."

Bala smiled, feeling a sense of warmth in his heart. "You don't have to thank me, Madame. I'm just glad I could help."

As Bala prepared to leave, Samir's mother, Madame Dupont, approached him with a warm smile. "Monsieur Riaz, I don't want you to leave just yet. You've been through so much with Samir, and I want to thank you properly."

Bala hesitated, unsure of what to say. He had been traveling under a false name, and he wasn't sure if he should stay.

But Madame Dupont's warm hospitality put him at ease. "Please, stay with us for a few days till the end of Ramzan fast. We have a spare room, and you're welcome to stay as long as you like."

Bala's heart swelled with gratitude. No one had shown him such kindness in a long time. He nodded, smiling. "Merci, Madame. I'd be happy to stay."

As he settled into the spare room, Bala felt a sense of peace wash over him. He had been running for so long, for his task, and now, he finally felt satisfied.

Over the next few days, Bala grew closer to Samir and his mother. They showed him the sights of Paris, and he marveled at the beauty of the city.

But as the days passed, Bala knew he couldn't stay forever. He had to face the consequences of his actions, and he couldn't keep running forever.

One evening, as they sat down to dinner, Madame Dupont turned to Bala with a curious expression. "Monsieur Riaz, I have to ask, what brings you to France? You're not from around here, are you?"

Bala's heart skipped a beat. He knew he had to be careful, but he also knew he couldn't keep lying forever.

Madame Dupont's question hung in the air, and Bala knew he had to think fast. He couldn't reveal his true identity as an Indian spy, not even to Samir's mother, who had been so kind to him.

But he also knew he couldn't keep lying. He had to come up with a convincing cover story, one that would satisfy Madame Dupont's curiosity without putting his mission at risk.

"I'm a...a businessman," Bala said finally, trying to sound as convincing as possible. "I was in Mecca for...for a conference, and I met Samir and his grandfather there."

Madame Dupont's eyes narrowed slightly, and Bala knew she wasn't entirely convinced. But she didn't press the issue, and instead, changed the subject.

As they finished dinner and the evening drew to a close, Bala couldn't shake off the feeling that he was living on borrowed time. He knew that his mission was far from over, and that he would have to return to his work as a spy soon.

But for now, he was content to stay with Samir and his mother, enjoying the peace and quiet of their little family.

Little did he know, however, that his presence in Paris had not gone unnoticed. A Pakistani agent, who had been tracking Bala's movements, had finally caught up with him.

And this agent was none other than the Pakistani officer Bala had been tracking to Mecca...

As the sun began to set, Madame Dupont, whose name was actually Yasmin, busied herself in the kitchen, preparing for Iftar. Bala, wanting to help, offered to assist her.

Together, they worked in comfortable silence, Bala learning about the various traditional dishes that Yasmin was preparing. As they worked, Yasmine couldn't help but steal glances at Bala, who was moving with ease in her kitchen.

As the call to prayer sounded, Yasmin and Bala sat down to break their fast together. The food was delicious, and Bala found himself feeling more and more at ease in Jasmine's presence.

As the night wore on, Yasmin began to open up to Bala, sharing stories about her past and her struggles as a single mother. Bala listened intently, finding himself drawn to her warmth and kindness.

But what Bala didn't know was that Yasmin was hiding a secret. She had been recruited by the Pakistani agent, who had been tracking Bala, to divert his attention away from his spying duties.

Yasmin's mission was to gain Bala's trust, to make him fall for her, and to keep him distracted from his work. But as she looked into Bala's eyes, she couldn't help but feel a pang of guilt.

Was she really just using him, or was she starting to develop real feelings for him?

CHAPTER THREE

As the night drew to a close, Bala thanked Yasmin for the delicious meal and the warm hospitality. Yasmin smiled, feeling a flutter in her chest.

"Anytime, Bala," she said, her voice barely above a whisper. "You're welcome to stay with me for as long as you need."

Bala smiled back, feeling a sense of gratitude towards Yasmin. He had no idea that he was walking into a trap, one that would test his loyalty, his duty, and his heart.

As the days passed, Yasmin found herself growing more and more comfortable around Bala. She had initially thought that he would be like other men, trying to take advantage of her vulnerability. But Bala proved to be different.

He was kind, gentle, and respectful. He played with Samir with a fondness that touched Yasmin's heart, even her abandoned husband has never played with his son which was over before two years. She began to feel a sense of gratitude towards him, and maybe even something more.

As Ramadan came to an end, Yasmin decided to test Bala's intentions. She offered herself to him, expecting him to take advantage of the situation. But Bala surprised her.

He looked at her with a deep sadness in his eyes and said, "Yasmin, I'm honored that you would even think of me in that way. But I could never take advantage of you. You're a strong, independent woman who's struggling to make a life for yourself and your son. I admire that about you."

Yasmine felt a sting of shame as Bala continued, "Sympathy can't create love, Yasmin. I feel pity for you, but I don't love you. And I would never want to take advantage of your vulnerability."

Yasmin felt tears prick at the corners of her eyes as she realized the truth. She had been trying to manipulate Bala, to use her charms to get him to do what she wanted. But Bala had seen right through her.

She felt a deep sense of shame and regret. She had underestimated Bala, and she had underestimated herself.

After two days, Yasmin withdrew from Bala, unsure of how to process her emotions. Bala, sensing her withdrawal, gave her space, but continued to care for Samir with the same kindness and devotion.

CHAPTER FOUR

Yasmin's voice trembled as she spoke to the Pakistani agent on the phone. "I couldn't find anything, I swear. He doesn't even carry a phone with him."

The agent's voice was cold and menacing. "Meet me at the shopping mall. We need to discuss this further."

Yasmin arrived at the mall, her heart racing with anxiety. The agent was already there, his eyes narrowing as he looked at her.

"You're not doing your job, Yasmin," he sneered. "It's already ten days passed, I think you're too close to him. You're falling for him, aren't you?"

Yasmin's eyes flashed with anger, but she tried to keep her cool. "No, of course not. I'm just trying to do my job."

But the agent wasn't convinced. "I don't believe you," he spat. "You're going to have to try harder if you want to see your son again."

Suddenly, Yasmin's eyes widened in horror as she saw the agent's men grab Samir and drag him away. She screamed and ran after them, but they were too fast. They sped away in a car, leaving Yasmin alone and desperate.

The agent turned to her, his eyes glinting with cruelty. "You have 24 hours to get me what I want. If you don't, you'll never see your son again."

Yasmin's world went dark as she realized the true extent of her predicament. She was trapped, and she had no way out.

Yasmine burst into the flat, tears streaming down her face. Bala, who was cooking in the kitchen, immediately turned off the stove and rushed to her side.

"What's wrong, Yasmin? Where's Samir?" he asked, concern etched on his face.

Yasmin collapsed onto the couch, sobbing uncontrollably and opened her secret to Bala.

"They took him, Bala. The Pakistani agent's men took him. They want me to get information from you, but I couldn't do it. I'm so sorry."

Bala's expression remained calm, but his eyes narrowed slightly. "What information do they want and where are they?" he asked his voice gentle and eager.

Yasmin took a deep breath, revealing everything - her arrangement with the Pakistani agent, her attempts to extract information from Bala, and her failure to do so.

As she spoke, Bala's face remained impassive, but his mind was racing. He had suspected that Yasmin might be working for someone, but he hadn't expected this.

When Yasmin finished speaking, Bala nodded thoughtfully. "Don't worry, Yasmine. We'll get Samir back. But first, we need to meet with the Pakistani agent."

Yasmin's eyes widened in surprise. "You're not angry with me?"

Bala smiled. "I'm not angry, Yasmin. But we need to play this carefully. Can you arrange a meeting with the agent?"

Yasmin nodded, still looking uncertain. Bala's calm demeanor had put her at ease, but she knew that she had betrayed him.

As they waited for the meeting to be arranged, Bala's mind was already racing ahead, planning his next move. He had played the innocent game perfectly, but now it was time to take control.

The Pakistani agent had no idea what was coming his way.

Usman, the Pakistani agent, had been tasked with two critical missions. First, he had to obtain the nuclear warhead details from the Turkish agent, which he had successfully done in Mecca.

His second task was to identify and track the Indian agent, Bala, who was operating under the alias Riaz Khan. Usman had been hired to gather intelligence on Bala's activities, specifically any information he might have obtained from the Israeli agent.

However, Usman had been unable to gather any concrete evidence of Bala's meetings with other agents. Frustrated and under pressure, he had hired Jasmine to extract information from Bala, unaware that Bala was actually playing a clever game of deception.

Now, as Usman prepared to meet with Jasmine and Bala, he was confident that he had finally trapped the Indian agent. But little did he know, Bala had been playing a long game, and his true mission was to steal the nuclear warhead details from Usman and sabotage Pakistan's nuclear missile mission against India.

Bala's eyes locked onto Usman's as they met in a deserted alleyway. Usman sneered, thinking he had the upper hand. But Bala's expression remained calm, his mind racing with the final stages of his plan.

<u>CHAPTER FIVE</u>

Bala's world went dark as he felt the sudden blow to the back of his head. He tried to turn around, but his body wouldn't respond. He heard Yasmin's screams, but they were distant, muffled.

As he fell to the ground, he saw Usman's face, twisted in a cruel smile. "Oh, finally, you're the one," Usman sneered, his eyes gleaming with triumph.

Bala tried to speak, but his words were slurred, indistinct. He saw Yasmin struggling in Usman's grasp, her eyes wild with fear.

And then, everything went black.

When Bala came to, he was lying in a dark, damp cell. His head throbbed with pain, and his body felt bruised and battered.

He struggled to sit up, but a wave of dizziness washed over him, forcing him back onto the cold stone floor.

As he lay there, he realized that he had been caught, that his mission had been compromised. But he also knew that he couldn't give up, not yet.

With a newfound determination, Bala began to think, to plan. He would escape, no matter what it took. He would complete his mission, no matter the cost.

But for now, he lay in the darkness, his mind racing with thoughts of escape, of revenge, of redemption.

Usman arrived with two accomplices, and a torch was shone in Bala's face. Bala didn't flinch, but slowly opened his eyes. Usman demanded to know what information Bala had received from the Israeli agent, promising to spare his life if he cooperated.

But Bala turned the tables, asking about the woman and her child. Usman sneered, saying they were safe, but their safety depended on Bala's willingness to talk.

Bala remained calm, revealing that he hadn't received the hard disk. "It's still in Mecca," he said, "with the travel agent who received it from the Israeli agent."

Usman's face turned beet red with rage as he processed Bala's words. "You're lying!" he spat, his voice echoing off the cold stone walls. "I know you received the hard disk. You're just trying to protect the Israeli agent."

Bala remained calm, his eyes fixed on Usman. "I'm telling you the truth. The hard disk is still in Mecca. If you don't believe me, go and check yourself."

Usman's anger boiled over, and he nodded to his accomplices. "Arrange for our departure to Mecca. Now."

As the two men scurried off to make the necessary arrangements, Usman turned back to Bala. "You're coming with us. And if we don't find that hard disk, you'll regret ever crossing me."

Bala nodded, a small smile playing on his lips. He knew he had bought himself some time, and he was ready to play out the next part of his plan.

As Usman's men returned with a car, Bala was dragged out of the cell and thrown into the backseat. Usman slid in beside him, a triumphant glint in his eye.

"You're a foolish man, Bala," Usman sneered. "You think you can outsmart me? I'll show you what happens to people who cross me."

Bala remained silent, his eyes fixed on the passing scenery as the car sped towards the city.

He knew the game was far from over, and he was ready to play his next move.

Bala's mind was racing with his new plan. He knew that he had to extract the nuclear warhead details from Usman and sabotage Pakistan's nuclear missile mission. And now, he also had to save Yasmin and her son Samir.

As they arrived at Usman's safehouse, Bala was relieved to see that Yasmin and Samir were being held there, under the watchful eyes of Usman's goons.

Bala was kept under close surveillance, but he was determined to use the time to his advantage. Since flight bookings to Mecca would take at least a day or two, Bala had a window of opportunity to search Usman's dwelling for any clues or information.

As he was led to his room, Bala took note of the layout of the safehouse, looking for any weaknesses or vulnerabilities. He knew that he would have to be careful, as Usman's men were likely to be watching his every move.

But Bala was a seasoned operative, and he was confident that he could find a way to gather the information he needed. And with Yasmin and Samir being held captive, he had even more motivation to succeed.

As he waited for the perfect moment to strike, Bala's eyes locked onto Yasmin, who was sitting in the corner of the room, her eyes fixed on him. He gave her a subtle nod, trying to reassure her that he was working on a plan to save them.

Yasmin's eyes flickered with hope, and Bala knew that he had to act fast. He was running out of time, and he knew that Usman's patience was wearing thin.

CHAPTER SIX

Bala's eyes remained fixed on the locker behind the sofa, his mind racing with possibilities. He was convinced that the data he needed was stored there.

As he waited for Usman to leave, Bala carefully observed the two men guarding him. They seemed relaxed, but Bala knew he couldn't underestimate them.

Yasmin, who had been cooking in the kitchen, was brought back to the room and tied up again. Bala watched as she struggled against her restraints, her eyes filled with desperation.

As the hours passed, Bala heard Usman preparing to leave. He listened intently as Usman instructed his men to keep a close eye on the prisoners.

As soon as Usman left, Bala knew it was time to act. He glanced at Yasmin and Samir, who were watching him with wide eyes.

With a subtle nod, Bala signaled to Yasmin that he was about to make his move. Yasmin's eyes flickered with understanding, and she nodded slightly.

Bala turned his attention to the two guards, who were now lounging on the sofa, oblivious to the danger lurking in front of them.

With a swift and silent movement, Bala sprang into action, taking down the first guard with a precise blow. The second guard was caught off guard, and Bala quickly overpowered him.

As the guards lay unconscious on the floor, Bala turned to Yasmin and Samir, a triumphant smile on his face.

"It's time to get out of here," he whispered, quickly untying Yasmin and Samir.

Yasmin's eyes shone with tears as she hugged her son tightly. "Thank you, Bala," she whispered.

Bala's expression turned serious. "We're not out of danger yet. We need to find that data and get out of here before Usman returns."

With a deep breath, Bala approached the locker behind the sofa, his heart racing with anticipation.

As Bala searched the locker, Yasmin's eyes clouded over, memories of her past flooding back. "I was just 15 when I met him," she began, her voice barely above a whisper. "He was a student of my father's, studying nuclear physics. He was charming, handsome, and attentive. I was young and naive, and I fell for him hard."

Bala's expression remained neutral, but his eyes betrayed a hint of sympathy. "What happened next?" he asked, his voice gentle.

Yasmin took a deep breath. "He seduced me, and then he convinced me to convert to Islam and marry him. My father was devastated, but I was too far gone to listen. I thought I was in love."

Bala's eyes narrowed. "And then?"

Yasmin's voice cracked. "He abandoned me, left me with nothing. And then this Pakistani agent, Usman, showed up. He was a friend of my husband's, and also a student of my father's. He promised to help me, to take care of me and Samir. But it was all a lie."

Bala's face hardened. "He used you to get to your father's research," he growled.

Yasmin nodded, tears streaming down her face. "I was so blind, so stupid. I didn't see it until it was too late."

Bala's expression softened. "You're not stupid, Yasmin. You were manipulated, used. But we're going to get out of this, together."

As Yasmin nodded, Bala's eyes locked onto the locker, his mind racing with the implications of what Yasmin had just told him. He knew that he had to find that data, no matter what it took.

Bala's eyes scanned the crowded street, his mind racing with the urgency of their mission. He spotted a browsing center nearby and quickly ushered Yasmin and Samir inside.

"Excuse me," Bala asked the manager, a bespectacled man with a curious expression. "We need to use a computer urgently."

The manager eyed Bala warily. "I need to see your ID, please."

Yasmin quickly intervened, producing her identity card from her bag. The manager scrutinized it before nodding and handing Bala a laptop.

As soon as Bala booted up the laptop, he inserted the drive he had recovered from the flat. The screen flickered to life, revealing a complex diagram of the India-Pakistan border.

Bala's eyes widened as he took in the shocking information. Thirty-two nuclear missiles, strategically placed along the Line of Control (LOC), were ready to be activated. But the activation code, provided by the Turkish manufacturing company, was still pending.

Usman's role in the negotiations became clear to Bala. He was the Pakistani agent tasked with securing the activation code, essentially holding the key to unleashing nuclear devastation on India.

Bala's face set in a determined expression. He knew he had to act fast, to prevent a catastrophic war between the two nations.

Bala quickly devised a plan to create a dummy document, exaggerating the nuclear missile deployment to four times the actual number, complete with a countdown timer. His goal was to deceive Usman into believing the fake plan was real.

Unbeknownst to Bala, the browsing center manager had been secretly monitoring his activities. As Bala opened the password-protected file and transferred it to a new drive, the manager's eyes widened with alarm.

The manager swiftly picked up his phone and dialed a number, whispering urgently to the person on the other end. "I think I've stumbled upon something big... Come quickly."

Meanwhile, Bala, Yasmin, and Samir exited the browsing center, unaware of the danger lurking nearby. Suddenly, a police wagon screeched to a halt outside, and officers poured out, surrounding them.

Bala's instincts kicked in, and he tried to hurry away, but the police officials were too quick. They pinned him to the ground, slapping handcuffs on his wrists. Yasmin and Samir were also detained, their faces filled with fear.

As the police dragged them away, Bala caught a glimpse of the browsing center manager watching from the shadows, a smug expression on his face.

Unbeknownst to Bala, Usman had orchestrated the trap, anticipating that Bala would bring the drive to the internet center. Usman's plan relied on the browsing center manager's cooperation, ensuring that the police would apprehend Bala and recover the drive.

However, Bala's quick thinking had allowed him to stay one step ahead. By creating a dummy plan on a new drive and dating it a month prior, he had cleverly deceived Usman.

When Usman arrived at the police station, he bribed the officials and conducted a thorough search of Bala. The drive was discovered hidden in Bala's undergarment, and Usman's eyes widened as he read the contents.

The dummy plan revealed an entirely different nuclear missile deployment strategy, one that was far more extensive and alarming. Usman's face turned pale as he realized the implications, and he immediately contacted his headquarters to abort the mission.

Bala's plan had worked. He had successfully deceived Usman and foiled the nuclear missile deployment. As he sat in his cell, a hint of a smile played on his lips. He knew that he had just prevented a catastrophic war between India and Pakistan.

But Bala's relief was short-lived. He knew that Usman would not give up easily, and that he would stop at nothing to achieve his goals. Bala's mission was far from over.

CHAPTER SEVEN

Bala's eyes closed, and he took a deep breath, feeling a sense of temporary relief wash over him. But he knew his mission was far from complete. He still needed to obtain the coordinates of Pakistan's nuclear missiles and transmit them back to India.

As he pondered his next move, Bala's thoughts turned to his impending release. He knew that getting out of the police station wouldn't be easy, especially with corrupt officials on Usman's payroll.

But Bala had anticipated this challenge. Before leaving the internet center, he had sent a cryptic email to the Indian embassy, informing them that his mission was half-accomplished and that he needed their assistance to complete the rest.

Now, as he sat in his cell, Bala heard the sound of raised voices and footsteps echoing through the police station. He recognized the authoritative tone of Indian officials, and a hint of a smile played on his lips.

The door to his cell swung open, and a tall, imposing figure in a crisp suit walked in. "Bala, you're coming with us," he said, his voice firm but reassuring.

Bala stood up, a sense of casual relief washing over him. He knew that the Indian officials would take care of the corrupt police officers and Usman's agents.

As he walked out of the cell, flanked by the Indian officials, Bala felt a sense of hope. He was one step closer to completing his mission and returning home.

But he knew that the real challenge lay ahead – getting the missile coordinates and transmitting them back to India without getting caught.

As they walked out of the police station, Bala turned to Yasmin and said, "We'll get you and Samir safely back to your flat. The embassy will provide protection."

But Yasmin shook her head, her eyes determined. "I don't want to go back to my flat. I want to come with you to India."

Bala's expression turned concerned. "Yasmin, it's not safe. My mission is complicated, and I couldn't guarantee your safety or Samir's."

But Yasmin's resolve only strengthened. "I'm not safe here either. I have no one, Bala. My husband abandoned me, and I'm just a pawn in Usman's game. I'll do anything to live a peaceful life with you in India."

Bala's face softened, but he knew he couldn't make promises he might not be able to keep. "Yasmin, please understand—"

But Yasmin cut him off, her voice firm. "I'll take the risk, Bala. I'll go to any extent to be with you and raise Samir as an Indian, away from all this chaos."

Bala's heart went out to her, but he knew he had to be realistic and she is almost half of his age and he is no suitor for her. He couldn't put Yasmin and Samir in harm's way, no matter how much he wanted to help them.

Bala knew he had to act swiftly. With the information from Usman's drive, he discovered that the Turkish company was waiting to hand over the pass codes to Pakistan. Bala had to reach

Turkey before Usman did, and he knew it wouldn't be an easy task.

As an Indian military engineer, crossing the border into Turkey would be impossible without arousing suspicion. But Bala had an idea. He requested the Indian embassy to make arrangements for him to travel to Turkey as a tourist, using a duplicate French passport.

The embassy, aware of the sensitive nature of Bala's mission, agreed to help. They created a duplicate French passport for Bala, listing him as a settler by marriage, taking advantage of the historical connection between France and India, particularly in Pondicherry.

With his new passport, Bala, along with Yasmin and Samir, would travel to Turkey as tourists. Yasmin's original French passport, with her maiden name Dupont, added credibility to their cover story.

As they prepared to leave, Bala felt a sense of relief wash over him. They had a solid plan in place, and with their new identities, they should be able to blend in seamlessly with the tourist crowd in Turkey.

But Bala knew that even with the best-laid plans, things could go wrong. He was aware of the risks involved, but he was determined to see his mission through, no matter what it took.

As the plane took off, Bala settled into his aisle seat, with Samir in the middle seat beside him. Yasmin, who had been assigned the window seat, surprised Bala by switching places with Samir.

As she sat down beside Bala, she smiled softly, her eyes shining with a sense of freedom. For the first time in five years, she had removed her scarf, letting her dark hair flow freely.

Bala's eyes met hers, and he smiled back, his heart warming to her gentle gesture. As the flight attendants began their safety demonstrations, Yasmin reached out and locked her fingers with Bala's.

The simple touch sent a spark of electricity through Bala's body. He felt a deep sense of connection to Yasmin, one that went beyond mere gratitude or friendship.

As the plane leveled off, Yasmin closed her eyes, a soft sigh escaping her lips. Bala watched her, his eyes drinking in the peaceful expression on her face.

For a moment, they just sat there, hands entwined, the hum of the engines and the gentle rocking of the plane lulling them into a sense of tranquility.

But Bala knew that their peace was fleeting. They still had a long way to go, and the dangers that lay ahead were very real.

As they stepped out of the airport, Bala's eyes widened in surprise. Large hoardings announcing the International Military Expo dominated the airport lounge. The expo's logo featured a stylized eagle, symbolizing Turkey's military prowess.

Bala's mind racing, he saw an opportunity. He could use the expo as a cover to gain access to Turkey's nuclear research center. By posing as an ambitious French citizen, he might be able to gather valuable information.

After checking into their hotel, Bala approached the tour operator in the lobby. "We're interested in exploring Istanbul's sights," he said, affecting a French accent. "What would you recommend?"

The tour operator smiled, handing Bala a brochure. "We have a special package that includes the Military Expo. It's a great opportunity to see the latest advancements in military technology."

Bala's eyes lit up. This was exactly the opening he needed. "That sounds perfect," he said, smiling. "We'll take the package."

After freshening up and enjoying a hearty breakfast, the trio set out for their sightseeing adventure. Bala's excitement grew as they approached the expo center. He knew that this was just the beginning of their mission.

As they entered the expo center, Bala's eyes scanned the crowds, taking in the various exhibits and displays. He spotted several high-ranking military officials and scientists mingling with the attendees.

Bala's mind racing, he began to formulate a plan. He would need to blend in, gather information, and make connections without arousing suspicion.

CHAPTER EIGHT

Bala, with Samir perched on his hip and Yasmin (Dupont) holding his elbow, approached the nuclear missile stall. He confidently introduced himself as a 3D model developer and freelancer, highlighting his extensive experience working with various companies worldwide.

As they walked through the stall, Bala's eyes widened in awe at the cutting-edge missile designs on display. He had never seen such advanced technology in India. Eager to learn more, Bala struck up a conversation with the stall manager.

To his surprise, the manager revealed himself to be the marketing head. Bala seized the opportunity, inquiring about potential design collaborations. The marketing manager, impressed by Bala's credentials, handed him a business card with the contact information of Mr. Aliyar, the head of the research and development wing.

With the valuable contact in hand, Bala promptly excused himself, eager to meet with Mr. Aliyar. As they walked away from the stall,

Yasmin leaned in, whispering, "You're doing great, Bala. We're getting close."

Bala smiled reassuringly, his mind racing with anticipation. He knew that meeting Mr. Aliyar could be the breakthrough they needed to uncover the secrets of Pakistan's nuclear missile program.

Bala's suspicions grew as he received the invitation to meet Prof. Aliyar at a restaurant instead of his research center. He couldn't shake off the feeling that something was off.

Unbeknownst to Bala, Usman had already arrived in Turkey and met with Prof. Aliyar. However, the professor had become cautious after learning that Bala had misled Usman with the fake missile deployment plan.

Prof. Aliyar's team was working tirelessly to complete the pass code assignment for the missile software program, which was expected to be finished by the next day.

The next morning, Bala met Prof. Aliyar at the agreed-upon location. As they sat down, Bala introduced Yasmin as his wife and mentioned her father, Prof. Lucas. Prof. Aliyar's expression changed dramatically, and he looked like he had seen a ghost.

"Prof. Lucas from University de Lorraine?" he asked, his voice trembling with excitement. Yasmin nodded, and Prof. Aliyar's face lit up with joy.

"Ah, he was my favorite professor! He taught me nuclear science, and I owe my career to him. I'm forever grateful to him," Prof. Aliyar exclaimed, his eyes shining with sincerity.

He turned to Bala and Yasmin, his expression determined. "I'll help you in any way I can. You're like family to me now."

Bala's eyes met Yasmin's, and they exchanged a hopeful glance. Maybe, just maybe, they had found an unexpected ally in Prof. Aliyar.

Bala decided to reveal his true intentions to Prof. Aliyar, explaining his mission to intercept the pass codes and prevent them from falling into Usman's hands. To his surprise, Prof. Aliyar didn't seem shocked or alarmed.

"I apologize for deceiving you earlier," Bala said, feeling a twinge of guilt.

Prof. Aliyar waved his hand dismissively. "No need to apologize, Bala. I appreciate your straightforwardness and innocence. You're not like the others who deal with Usman."

Prof. Aliyar's expression turned serious. "Speaking of which, Usman is here, watching us, and you're under threat. We must keep this meeting casual, and you should leave now."

Bala nodded, understanding the gravity of the situation.

"I'll help you, but I must protect myself and my government," Prof. Aliyar continued. "I'll schedule a meeting with Usman for tomorrow afternoon, same place, same time. But I want you to come earlier, with some... hired help. Take the software from me, and I'll claim I was coerced."

Bala's eyes narrowed, understanding the plan.

"One more thing," Prof. Aliyar added. "Don't bring Dupont and the child tomorrow. It's not safe. And I advise you to change your hotel suite tonight, just in case."

Bala nodded, gratitude welling up inside him. "Thank you, Professor. I won't forget your help."

With a final nod, Bala left the meeting, his mind racing with the plan for the next day. He knew it wouldn't be easy, but with Prof. Aliyar's help, he might just have a chance to succeed.

<u>CHAPTER NINE</u>

Bala took every precaution to ensure his safety and the success of the mission. He changed hotels at midnight, constantly checking to see if he was being followed.

The next day, he hired local men to pose as goons, equipped with dummy pistols and face masks. They arrived at the designated meeting spot earlier than scheduled, waiting for Prof. Aliyar's arrival.

As the professor's black sedan came into view, Bala gave a nod to his accomplices. They sprang into action, surrounding Prof. Aliyar with masked faces and pointing dummy guns at him.

Bala swiftly took the software drive from the professor, double-checking their plan on the nearby CCTV cameras. But just as they were about to make their escape, a sudden, unexpected sound pierced the air - the sound of gunfire.

Bala's eyes widened in horror as he saw Prof. Aliyar's chest swell with blood. Without hesitation, he took charge of the situation, yelling at his accomplices to flee.

As they scattered, Bala rushed to Prof. Aliyar's car, pulling the driver out and taking the wheel. He sped away from the scene, the sound of sirens growing fainter in the distance.

Bala's eyes darted between the rearview mirror and the road ahead, his heart racing with every passing second. Two cars were hot on his tail, their drivers determined to catch up.

"Professor, are you okay?" Bala asked, his voice laced with concern.

Prof. Aliyar winced in pain, his face pale. "I...I think so. Just get us out of here."

Bala pressed his kerchief against the professor's bullet wound, trying to stem the bleeding. He floored it, weaving through the crowded streets and sending pedestrians scrambling for safety.

Prof. Aliyar's voice grew weaker, but his words were laced with urgency. "Bala, leave me. Escape. You can't risk being caught."

But Bala refused to abandon the professor. "I won't leave you, Professor. I'll get you to a clinic, and once you're safe, I'll leave."

Prof. Aliyar's eyes locked onto Bala's, filled with a deep sense of responsibility. "You don't understand, Bala. If we're caught together, it will compromise everything. Our contract with the Pakistani government...it's too sensitive."

Bala's grip on the wheel tightened. He understood the stakes, but he couldn't bring himself to abandon the professor.

After a few tense moments, Bala confirmed they'd shaken off their pursuers. He spotted a small clinic and pulled over, rushing Prof. Aliyar inside.

But their relief was short-lived. The doctors refused to treat the professor's bullet wound, citing the need to report it to the police.

Bala's mind racing, he knew they had to act fast. He couldn't let the police get involved, not now, when they were so close to their goal.

Prof. Aliyar's eyes fluttered open, and he gazed up at Bala, a faint smile on his lips. "Thank you, Bala...thank you for saving my life."

Bala's eyes welled up with emotion as he held the professor's hand. "You're safe now, Professor. That's all that matters."

Prof. Aliyar's voice was weak but filled with gratitude. "This humanity, Bala...this is why you Indians stand tall from the crowd. I appreciate you, Bala. You've shown me that even in the darkest of times, there's still hope."

Bala's heart swelled with pride, but he knew he couldn't linger. "I'll leave now, Professor. You need to rest."

With a heavy heart, Bala bid farewell to Prof. Aliyar and headed back to his hotel. But as he approached his suite, a chill ran down his spine.

The door was open, and the room was vacant. A note on the door sent a shiver down Bala's spine: "Usman always wins."

Bala's eyes scanned the room, his mind racing with the implications. Usman had found him, and Yasmin and Samir were nowhere to be seen.

CHAPTER TEN

Bala's anger boiled over as he rushed to the reception, demanding to know what had happened to his wife and child. The receptionist, taken aback by Bala's urgency, explained that a friend had taken them away just an hour ago, leaving behind an address.

Seething with rage, Bala thought about Usman's relentless pursuit. He regretted not eliminating him in France, instead of just misleading him.

With a deep breath, Bala composed himself and returned to his room. He inserted the software drive into the hotel's laptop and accessed the contents. However, he refrained from transmitting the details to his project head, citing the unsecured connection.

Instead, Bala memorized the four-digit pass codes for all thirty-two missiles. He then deliberately entered false pass codes, rewrote the drive, and pocketed it.

Bala knew Usman would likely follow the same protocol, carrying the pass codes by hand to Pakistan rather than transmitting them. This realization gave Bala a sense of relief; he had time to rescue Yasmin, Samir, and himself.

With a newfound sense of determination, Bala set out to track down Usman and rescue his loved ones. The stakes were higher than ever, but Bala was ready to face whatever challenges lay ahead.

Bala's taxi pulled up short of the address, a hotel nestled beside the Pakistani embassy. He got out, eyes scanning the surroundings, and made his way to a nearby restaurant. From a discreet table, he kept watch on the hotel, his mind racing with plans to rescue Yasmin and Samir.

However, Bala's instincts told him he wasn't alone. He noticed two men sitting next to his table, their eyes fixed on him with an air of suspicion. One wrong move, and they'd alert Usman.

Determined to maintain his cover, Bala ordered a cool drink and began sipping it casually. He took a leisurely stroll around the restaurant, using the opportunity to observe his followers without arousing their suspicion.

As he walked back to his table, Bala subtly removed the software drive from his coat pocket and placed it on the table, watching his followers' reactions out of the corner of his eye. Their expressions remained neutral, but Bala detected a flicker of interest in their eyes.

Bala smiled to himself, knowing he'd sent a deliberate message. He was in control, and his captors would soon realize that.

With the drive still on the table, Bala continued his charade, waiting for the perfect moment to make his next move. His eyes locked onto the hotel, his mind focused on rescuing Yasmin and Samir.

Bala's plan was to lure his followers to a secluded spot, and the restroom seemed like the perfect place. He casually asked the receptionist for directions to the restroom, knowing his followers would trail behind.

As he entered the restroom, Bala left the door ajar, inviting them in. He quickly slipped into the WC chamber, closing the door behind him.

His followers took the bait, entering the restroom and positioning themselves at the urinals. Bala sprang into action, smashing the first man's head against the wall, rendering him unconscious.

The second man rushed to his aid, but Bala was ready. With a swift kick, he sent the man crashing to the far end of the restroom, knocking him out cold.

With his followers neutralized, Bala exited the restroom, making his way to the hotel suite where Yasmin and Samir were being held. The receptionist had given him the room number: 203.

Meanwhile, Usman paced back and forth in the hotel suite, growing increasingly restless. He hadn't heard from his men, and the silence was unnerving. Yasmin and Samir sat quietly, their eyes fixed on Usman, who seemed to be waiting for something – or someone.

Bala knocked on the door, and Usman answered, a sly smile spreading across his face. He stepped aside, allowing Bala to enter, and deliberately left the door open, expecting his men to arrive soon.

"Release Yasmin and Samir," Bala demanded, his eyes scanning the room.

Usman sneered, his hand extended. "First, hand over the software drive."

Bala's gaze fell upon the personal laptop on the table, its screen glowing with an open secure connection. He knew he had to destroy it to prevent Usman from checking the pass codes.

With a fierce cry, Bala grabbed the nearby table clock and hurled it at the laptop, shattering the screen. Usman's eyes widened in terror as he stumbled backward and still he had the embassy nearby for access.

"Where are they?" Bala thundered, his anger boiling over.

Usman, still shaken, pointed down the hall. "They're safe, in room 204. I swear, just give me the drive."

Bala's eyes narrowed. "I want to see them first."

Usman hesitated, then led Bala to room 204. Yasmin and Samir were indeed safe, though visibly shaken.

With a surge of relief, Bala handed the software drive to Usman, who snatched it greedily. Bala quickly gathered Yasmin and Samir, and together they fled the room, hurrying out of the hotel as fast as they could.

As they emerged into the bright sunlight, Bala knew they weren't out of danger yet. Usman's men could still be lurking nearby, and the Pakistani embassy was just a stone's throw away.

Bala knew he had to escape Turkey and find a safe way back to India. Without a plan, he decided to return to France, where he had established connections. He contacted the French embassy, explaining his situation, and received immediate aid from the embassy officials.

Upon landing in Paris, Bala felt a sense of relief wash over him. He checked into a hotel near the Indian embassy and arranged for visas for Yasmin (Dupont) and Samir (Leon). The embassy personnel efficiently handled the process, and the visas were expected to be ready within two days.

However, Bala knew that time was running out. Usman would likely discover that the pass codes had been changed, and his reaction would be furious.

Meanwhile, in Turkey, Usman was struggling to understand why the pass codes he had sent to his headquarters in Islamabad weren't working. The system refused to activate, and Usman's anger grew. He felt cheated by Bala and was determined to track him down.

With the help of the Pakistani embassy, Usman discovered that Bala had fled to France. His eyes narrowed, and a sinister smile spread across his face. The hunt was far from over.

<u>CHAPTER ELEVEN</u>

Bala anticipated that Usman would exploit Pakistan's strong ties with Turkey to track him down in France. To throw Usman off his trail, Bala devised a plan to take a circuitous route to India, one that would deny Usman any potential assistance.

He decided to fly to England, knowing that Usman would be confused by this unexpected move. With a two-day window before Usman could react, Bala boarded a flight to England.

The next day, Bala returned to France by train, leaving behind a trail that would lead Usman on a wild goose chase in England. Usman, expecting Bala to be in England, would be searching for him in the wrong place, without any local support.

Bala's plan was working, and he had bought himself some valuable time. He could now focus on getting Yasmin and Samir to India safely, while Usman was busy searching for him in England.

But Bala knew that Usman wouldn't give up easily. He would eventually realize his mistake and regroup. Bala had to stay one step ahead of his adversary if he wanted to protect his loved ones and complete his mission.

Bala's journey didn't end with escaping Usman's clutches. He had a secret mission to complete, one that had been in the works since his encounter with Usman in Mecca.

Instead of taking a direct flight to Delhi, Bala booked a flight to Israel, a move that would throw Usman off his trail once again.

Yasmin (Dupont) was perplexed when she discovered their destination. "Israel? What's going on, Bala?" she asked, her eyes narrowing with suspicion.

Bala smiled mischievously. "You'll see. Just be patient."

Upon landing in Jerusalem, Dupont's curiosity turned to astonishment. "What's the plan, Bala?" she pressed, but he just chuckled and said, "You'll see for yourself."

Bala's mission was to meet with Professor Abraham, the head of Israel's Overseas Nuclear Program. He had to hand over the modified pass codes to the professor, who would then use them to deactivate the missiles and potentially turn them against Pakistan.

This was the final piece of Bala's plan, one that would ensure Pakistan's nuclear threat was neutralized. But he had to keep it under wraps, even from Dupont, to maintain the element of surprise.

As they made their way through the bustling streets of Jerusalem, Bala's senses were on high alert. He knew Usman could still be lurking, waiting for his chance to strike.

Professor Abraham's voice was laced with concern when Bala informed him of his arrival. "Bala, what's behind the delay? You were supposed to be here weeks ago."

Bala reassured him, "I'll explain everything in person, Professor. It's a long story."

The two agreed to meet in the evening, and when Professor Abraham saw Dupont accompanying Bala, his expression turned alarmed.

As Bala recounted the entire story, including Prof. Aliyar's injury and their narrow escape from Usman, Professor Abraham's face reflected a mix of shock, sympathy, and admiration.

Dupont, listening intently, felt a pang of guilt for underestimating Bala's abilities. She wondered if she had been a match for him all along.

Bala handed over the pass codes, neatly written on a piece of paper that he had memorized. Professor Abraham's eyes widened as he took the paper, his mind racing with the implications.

With the codes in hand, Professor Abraham led them through the tight security of Israel's Defense Research Wing, Dupont marveling at the advanced technology and secrecy surrounding them.

As they entered Professor Abraham's office, Dupont turned to Bala, her voice barely above a whisper. "I had no idea...am I even a match for you?"

Bala's smile was enigmatic. "We make a good team, Dupont. That's all that matters."

But Dupont's eyes sparkled with a newfound respect for Bala, and a hint of curiosity about what other secrets he might be hiding.

CHAPTER TWELVE

Professor Abraham and his team of scientists worked tirelessly in the control room, using Prof. Aliyar's software to retrieve the critical data. After several tense moments, they finally managed to reframe the software and obtain the coordinates of all thirty-two missiles.

Bala, with his expertise as a nuclear engineer, took center stage. His primary task was to determine the type of fuel used in the missiles. If it was uranium, his job would be significantly easier, as they could divert the missiles into the Arabian Ocean.

Since the missiles were not intercontinental, aiming for the Indian Ocean was out of the question. Bala also needed to assess the level of fuel used. If it was a hydrazine mix, the missiles would have intercontinental capabilities, which would complicate matters.

However, after checking the fuel system, Bala breathed a sigh of relief. The missiles used only enriched uranium, which meant they were not intercontinental. Pakistan's nuclear program was still in its infancy, and they didn't possess the technology for intercontinental missiles.

With this critical information, Bala and Professor Abraham's team could now focus on diverting the missiles into the Arabian Ocean, rendering them harmless. The tension in the room began to dissipate, replaced by a sense of determination and purpose.

But as they delved deeper into the diversion process, Bala couldn't shake off the feeling that Usman was still out there, waiting for his chance to strike.

Bala quickly informed the Indian Embassy and Indian Coast Guard via radio, warning them to alert fishing vessels to move away from the coast and to check for any passenger or navy patrol vessels in the target area.

Professor Abraham turned to Bala with a mischievous glint in his eye. "Bala, can't we divert the missiles into Pakistan itself?"

Bala's expression turned solemn. "No, Professor. Pakistanis are my old brothers and sisters. We've just been partitioned for seventy-five years. I won't be a part of causing harm to innocent civilians."

Dupont's eyes welled up with tears as she listened to Bala's words. She was moved by his compassion and humanity, realizing that Bala was more than just a brilliant engineer – he was a kind and empathetic soul.

Professor Abraham nodded in appreciation. "You're a true humanitarian, Bala. I respect that." He entered the pass codes, targeting the missiles towards the Arabian Ocean.

As they waited for the missiles to be diverted, Bala's mind wandered to the amount of fuel used in the missiles. He thought to himself, "If this fuel were to be used to construct a nuclear power station, it would solve Pakistan's electricity crisis for five years."

Bala's thoughts reflected his concern for the well-being of the Pakistani people, despite the animosity between their governments. He hoped that one day, the two nations could put aside their differences and work towards a more peaceful and prosperous future.

General Alam Khan's face turned beet red as he witnessed the coordinates changing automatically at the Islamabad Defence Headquarters. He swiftly ordered his scientists to investigate the cause of the breach. Scientist Ibrahim sprang into action, tracking down the source of the anomaly. To his astonishment, he discovered that the system was being controlled from Israel [1].

Ibrahim rushed back to General Alam Khan, urging him to contact Usman to understand the situation. Upon reaching Usman, the general was met with helplessness. Usman explained that he was in Turkey, attempting to deactivate the software, but to no avail. The gravity of the situation intensified as General Alam Khan noticed the countdown had begun, with only six hours left on the clock.

The Pakistan Air Force Headquarters, located in E-9, Islamabad, is the central hub for the country's air defense operations [2]. The National Defence University, Islamabad, also plays a crucial role in the nation's defense strategy [3]. However, in this scenario, the defense headquarters was faced with an unprecedented crisis, with the control of their systems compromised by an external entity.

General Alam Khan's plan to convince the Prime Minister to announce a missile test to showcase Pakistan's capability to launch thirty-two missiles simultaneously was met with resistance. The Prime Minister was hesitant, fearing the public backlash due to the massive tax burden it would impose on citizens.

The situation escalated when the Prime Minister, unable to convince the General to stop the test, was threatened by General Alam Khan, who assured him that he would take over the government if anything went wrong [1].

Despite the Prime Minister's reservations, Pakistan's Prime Minister Nizamudin went on air to inform the nation about the impending missile test, framing it as a celebration of the country's military prowess. This move was likely intended to garner public support and distract from the underlying tensions within the government.

Bala and Prof. Abraham couldn't help but burst out laughing as they watched the Pakistani Prime Minister confirm the missile launch timing on live television. This unexpected move gave them an opening to add to the chaos.

Since Prof. Abraham could manipulate the countdown, they decided to delay the timing by an hour, setting it to seven hours. This change sent General Alam Khan's anger into overdrive. He ordered the Prime Minister to refrain from sharing any further information about the timing, but the Prime Minister refused, citing the need for transparency with the Pakistani people.

The situation escalated quickly, with General Alam Khan placing the Prime Minister under house arrest and seizing control of the media. The General also ordered a complete lockdown of the city, further heightening the tensions [1].

Prof. Aliyar, despite being threatened by Usman, attempted to convince him that retracing the software was impossible. He explained that the base program was Israeli, making it difficult for him to alter it.

Usman, however, was unforgiving. He placed a gun to Prof. Aliyar's forehead, giving him an ultimatum: retrace the software within an hour, or face death.

With his life hanging in the balance, Prof. Aliyar sent a desperate signal to Prof. Abraham using calligraphy. He begged Prof. Abraham to open the gateway of the software for just ten minutes, promising not to alter the launch program.

Prof. Aliyar's message was a cry for help, and he hoped that Prof. Abraham would understand the gravity of his situation. With time running out, Prof. Aliyar's life depended on Prof. Abraham's response.

CHAPTER THIRTEEN

Prof. Abraham cleverly gave limited access to Prof. Aliyar every hour, making it seem like he was trying his best to cooperate with Usman. Meanwhile, in Pakistan, news of the missile launch sparked widespread protests. People took to the streets, outraged by the government's decision to spend billions of rupees on a mission that would essentially be a waste, given the current economic struggles and inflation.

The situation escalated when General Alam Khan banned all TV channels and arrested journalists in an attempt to suppress the news. However, this move only fueled the fire, with the learned youth taking to the streets in groups, demanding answers from the government. They felt betrayed, claiming that the government had kept them in the dark for too long and was now hiding something [1].

As the protests engulfed Pakistan, General Alam Khan's situation grew increasingly dire. With only four hours left before the launch, his army struggled to maintain control over the local population.

Frustrated and desperate, the General lashed out at Usman, labeling him useless and ordering him to return from Turkey. Abandoning his reliance on Usman, General Alam Khan took matters into his own hands and contacted the Israel Defence Research, demanding to speak with the team head.

Prof. Abraham was swiftly summoned by security, and Bala, anticipating the call, waited patiently alongside Dupont and Leon. While Leon played games on a desktop computer, Dupont kept a watchful eye over him.

Upon entering the control room, Prof. Abraham informed Bala about General Alam Khan's plea to stop the launch. Bala's expression remained calm, but his mind was racing with the implications of the General's request.

With conviction, Bala stated that he couldn't make a decision alone, as it involved the security of the nation. He requested to speak directly with General Alam Khan to outline his conditions.

Prof. Abraham arranged for the call, but before connecting, he made it clear to the General that Bala's conditions must be accepted without question. Moreover, Bala demanded that the actions taken would be live telecast to him, the General, and the entire nation, ensuring transparency and accountability.

General Alam Khan's anger reached a boiling point when he was forced to accept conditions from Bala, a civilian and an enemy national. He has never taken orders from a civilian of his own nation and despite his frustration, he controlled his emotions and accepted the conditions without negotiation. Bala's gentle tone didn't ease the General's tension as he outlined the conditions, which included dismantling the missile, separating its nuclear fuel tank, and preparing for the arrival of Indian helicopters [1].

The conditions were broadcasted to the Air Force headquarters in New Delhi, prompting arrangements for 32 helicopters to collect the nuclear fuel and store it in India. Furthermore, Bala stipulated that a nuclear power plant be constructed in a selected location in Pakistan, with the nuclear fuel to be returned to Pakistan once the plant was operational.

The General's blood pressure surged upon hearing these demands, but he prioritized maintaining peace in the country and reluctantly accepted the conditions. This decision was likely influenced by the understanding that unmanaged anger can have severe consequences, including increased blood pressure, heart rate, and cardiovascular risk.

Bala continued to dictate the terms, instructing General Alam Khan to announce the abortion of the nuclear missile test mission to the Pakistani nation. The nuclear fuel would be redirected to a newly planned nuclear power plant in Abbottabad, promising citizens a 50% reduction in electricity charges for the next five years. This move was expected to boost industrialization and economic growth in Pakistan.

The General was left with no choice but to comply with Bala's demands, effectively putting the Pakistani government at the mercy of an "enemy civilian." This turn of events was a significant blow to Pakistan's military and political establishment, highlighting the country's vulnerability to external pressures.

General Alam Khan was surprised that Bala didn't mention the Pakistan-occupied Kashmir issue, a topic he had expected would be a key demand.

Following the General's instructions, the Pakistani nuclear scientist team sprang into action, rapidly dismantling the missile system within the one-hour time frame. The countdown timer was put on hold, displaying four hours remaining.

Simultaneously, the Indian Air Force swiftly deployed 32 helicopters from various locations across India stretching from Pune to Kashmir to collect the nuclear fuel from Pakistan's missile launch pads. The helicopters were likely equipped with specialized containers to safely transport the nuclear fuel, ensuring minimal risk of radiation exposure or environmental contamination.

Prof. Abraham was amazed by Bala's diplomatic maneuvering, exclaiming, "You've brought the General to his knees!" However, Bala remained humble, requesting Prof. Abraham to refrain from using phrases that might disrespect the General's position.

As per Bala's conditions, the Indian helicopters were deployed, and the fuel portions of the missiles were dismantled and lifted directly from all the deployment stations across Pakistan. General Alam Khan was visibly upset, but the people of Pakistan were overjoyed upon hearing the news on live television.

The announcement of the aborted missile test and the promise of reduced electricity charges brought a sense of relief and optimism to the Pakistani populace. The streets, which had been filled with protests just hours before, were now filled with celebrations and cheers.

General Alam Khan seethed with resentment over the events that had unfolded, feeling humiliated and betrayed by Bala's clever maneuvering. Seeking vengeance, he ordered a secret assassination operation through his intelligence wing, tasking Col. Rahman Khan with the mission.

Col. Rahman Khan swiftly sprang into action, gathering intelligence on Bala's next move. He discovered that Bala planned to leave Israel the following day with his newly adopted family on a separate, specially arranged flight. The Pakistani public and the Indians remained unaware of Bala's pivotal role in sabotaging Pakistan's nuclear missile plan.

Col. Rahman Khan devised a plan to launch a missile attack on the Israeli flight carrying Bala. He informed General Alam Khan of his strategy, who emphasized the importance of vigilance and personal involvement to ensure the operation's success. The General cautioned Col. Rahman Khan not to repeat the mistakes of Usman, implying that he should be more effective and reliable in executing the task.

CHAPTER FOURTEEN

Bala expressed his gratitude to Prof. Abraham for his cooperation in sabotaging Pakistan's nuclear missile plan. Prof. Abraham acknowledged that without Bala's swift action and willingness to risk his life, the mission would not have been successful.

Dupont, who had grown close to Bala, felt a sense of pride and joy, envisioning a new life with him in India. She dreamed of marrying Bala according to his customs and traditions, eager to spend the rest of her life by his side. Unaware of the dangers that lay ahead, Dupont, Bala, and Leon left for a guest house in the defense area, where they spent a peaceful evening together.

In a moment of introspection with teary eyes, Dupont hugged and apologized again for her past actions in France. Bala reassured her, advising her not to dwell on the past, acknowledging that his task had never been easy.

That night, after Bala had left, Prof. Abraham retrieved the CCTV footage of his conversations with Bala. He selected two specific recordings: one where Bala had urged him not to divert the missile towards Pakistani civilians, considering them his brothers and sisters separated by political circumstances, and another where Bala had shown respect to General Alam Khan by not emphasizing that he had been brought to his knees.

Prof. Abraham sent these recordings to General Alam Khan, providing a glimpse into Bala's compassionate and respectful nature.

Meanwhile, General Alam Khan was eagerly awaiting dawn, anticipating the execution of his plan to eliminate Bala. He was confident that the outcome would be in his favor.

As the General prepared for the night, his assistant informed him of an email from Israel, which required a password to access. Upon inquiring about the document, the assistant revealed that it was a video clip. However, the General decided to postpone viewing it until morning, considering it too late to attend to it.

Bala gently woke up Dupont early in the morning, instructing her not to disturb Leon, as he would carry the child in his arms. Dupont playfully responded that she shouldn't have been awakened either and should be carried in his arms as well.

Bala was charmed by her romantic approach and affectionately hugged her, kissing her forehead. He then reminded her to get ready within half an hour, as they needed to arrive at the airfield within the next hour.

Dupont felt privileged and excited to be traveling with Bala on a private Air Force flight. As they made their way to the flight, she requested to take a picture with him. Bala agreed, and they captured a moment together, creating a lasting memory.

Meanwhile, Col. Rahman Khan was poised to launch the missile, gathering the flight route from Jerusalem to New Delhi. He planned the attack for when the flight would be over the Arabian Sea, approximately 300 miles away from Karachi. Satisfied with his plan, he informed General Alam Khan, who confirmed the details.

As Col. Rahman Khan set the countdown timer, he inquired about the type of attack: manual or automatic. He emphasized that an automatic attack would be irreversible and couldn't be aborted once the countdown started.

General Alam Khan, still seething from the humiliation he suffered the day before, responded in a fierce tone, ordering Col. Rahman Khan to never abort the mission, even if he himself were to change his mind. The General's anger boiled over, and he violently threw his phone to pieces.

General Alam Khan's assistant entered his chambers, submitting the day's chores, including the video clip from Israel. The General lit a cigar and entered the password to play the video.

As he watched the footage, he was left speechless. He replayed the video multiple times, struggling to believe his eyes. But it was too late; the events had already unfolded.

The General urgently summoned Col. Rahman Khan to his chambers. As Col. Rahman arrived, he was shown the video, and his expression mirrored the General's astonishment. The General's words trailed off, his anger melting into agony.

His cigar dropped from his lips as he exclaimed, "Col. Rahman, is there any chance...?" Col. Rahman understood the General's gesture and replied, "It was set to automatic, sir. There are only ten minutes left before the missile intercepts the target."

As the flight soared over the Arabian Sea, Bala pointed out the breathtaking view to Dupont. He closed his eyes, exhaling a sigh of relief, and Dupont snuggled closer, holding his elbow and leaning against his shoulders.

Suddenly, the pilot's urgent voice crackled over the radio, warning of an incoming missile. Bala sprang into action, quickly securing parachutes for Dupont, Leon, and himself. Since

Leon was sleepy, Bala attached their parachutes together. The pilot ejected them all just in time, mere seconds before the missile struck the plane, shattering it into pieces in mid-air.

Bala's parachute was damaged by a piercing piece of debris, causing him to plummet faster. He landed on Dupont's parachute, and as he slid down, he grasped her rope. But to his horror, he discovered that a shattered piece of the plane had pierced Dupont's heart, and she was bleeding profusely in the air.

The pilot, who had managed to grab hold of Leon, signaled to Bala that they were safe, and inquired about Bala and Dupont's situation.

Bala, devastated by Dupont's bleeding chest, hugged her tightly. The single parachute was struggling to support their combined weight. Dupont, with a staggering voice, urged Bala to remove her parachute and prioritize Leon's safety, acknowledging that she wouldn't survive.

Bala, who had secretly harbored feelings for Dupont since their first meeting in Paris, finally confessed his love for her. Despite their significant age difference, he couldn't imagine living without her.

As they plummeted faster towards the ocean, Bala expressed his deep affection for Dupont, and they shared a final, poignant kiss. With a heavy heart, Bala took out his Swiss knife and cut the ropes of their parachute, surrendering to their fate as they hurtled towards the waves.

Col. Rahman's assistant informed him that the mission had been a success. However, General Alam Khan's reaction was unexpected. He removed his cap and tossed it onto a nearby table, saying, "Yes, it was a success for Bala. He succeeded in teaching us humanity, and we failed him."

Col. Rahman, sensing the General's distress, discreetly left him alone.

Before resigning from his duty, General Alam Khan took several unprecedented steps. He ordered the release of all politicians from house arrest and drafted a historic letter to the United Nations, with a copy addressed to India.

In the letter, he expressed Pakistan's desire to merge with India, forming a unified nation, Akhand Bharat. He declared that this union would bring an end to the Kashmir dispute, militancy, and the longstanding enmity between the two nations.

After sealing the letter, General Alam Khan sent it to both Pakistani and Indian media outlets. He then dispatched a search team to rescue Leon (Samir), intending to care for the child for the rest of his life.

With a sense of closure, General Alam Khan exited his office, carrying a single suitcase containing his belongings. He handed over the keys to the security personnel, bid them farewell, and walked away from his former life, leaving behind the weight of his past actions.

THANKING MESSAGE

This is my second novella after Neng sari. The last period rests heavy on this page. "Thank you," I wrote, a final, almost perfunctory gesture. And now it's done. The fourth book, a novella, purely fiction, any resemblance to any character is purely a coincidence. It is a culmination of years of stolen moments, late nights fueled by lukewarm coffee, and a persistent, nagging voice in my head, is finally out there. It's a strange feeling, this mix of relief and a quiet kind of ache.

I lean back in my worn armchair, the reading lamp casting a warm, yellow glow on the stack of pages beside me. This isn't the end, of course. The next installments are already forming in my mind, a chaotic, vibrant tangle of characters and plots. But this one, the first, feels different. It's a debut, a leap into the unknown.

I glance at the bottom of the last page, where I've left my email and WhatsApp details: balajinadar09@gmail.com and +919791048441. A small, hopeful offering in the form of feed back. I'm not just an author sending a book into the void; I'm reaching out, inviting connection, hoping someone out there will see themselves in these stories as I saw them while writing. It's terrifying and thrilling, this vulnerability. But above all, it's sincere. Thank you, truly, for reading.